THE FIRST BOOK OF MEZZO-SOPRANO/ALTO SOLOS

compiled by Joan Frey Boytim

G. SCHIRMER, Inc.

DISTRIBUTED BY

HAL•LEONARD®
CORPORATION
7777 W. BLUEMOUND RD. P.O. BOX 13819 MILWAUKEE, WI 53213

PREFACE

Repertoire for the beginning voice student, whether teenager, college student, or adult, always poses a great challenge for the voice teacher because of the varied abilities and backgrounds the students bring to the studio. This series of books for soprano, mezzo-soprano and alto, tenor, and baritone and bass provides a comprehensive collection of songs suitable for first and second year students of any age, but is compiled with the needs of the young singer in mind.

In general, students' first experiences with songs are crucial to their further development and continued interest. Young people like to sing melodious songs with texts they can easily understand and with accompaniments that support the melodic line. As the student gains more confidence, the melodies, the texts, and the accompaniments can be more challenging. I have found that beginning students have more success with songs that are short. This enables them to overcome the problems of musical accuracy, diction, tone quality, proper technique, and interpretation without being overwhelmed by the length of the song.

Each book in this series includes English and American songs, spirituals, sacred songs, and an introduction to songs in Italian, German, French and Spanish. Many students study Spanish in the schools today, and most studio volumes do not include songs in this language; therefore, we have included two for each voice type.

Several songs in the collections have been out of print in recent years, while others have been previously available only in sheet form. Special care has been taken to avoid duplication of a great deal of general material that appears in other frequently used collections. These new volumes, with over thirty songs in each book, are intended to be another viable choice of vocal repertoire at a very affordable price for the teacher and student.

Each book contains several very easy beginning songs, with the majority of the material rated easy to moderately difficult. A few songs are quite challenging musically, but not strenuous vocally, to appeal to the student who progresses very rapidly and who comes to the studio with a great deal of musical background.

In general, the songs are short to medium in length. The ranges are very moderate, yet will extend occasionally to the top and the bottom of the typical voice. The majority of the accompaniments are not difficult, and are in keys that should not pose major problems. The variety of texts represented offers many choices for different levels of individual student interest and maturity.

In closing, I wish to thank Richard Walters at Hal Leonard Publishing for allowing me to be part of this effort to create this new series of vocal collections. We hope that these books will fill a need for teachers and students with suitable, attractive and exciting music.

Joan Frey Boytim

CONTENTS

4   AMERICAN LULLABY   Gladys Rich

8   L'ANNEAU D'ARGENT (The Silver Ring)   Cécile Chaminade

12   DIE BEKEHRTE (The Converted One)   Max Stange

16   DER BLUMENSTRAUSS (The Nosegay)   Felix Mendelssohn

20   THE CHERRY TREE   Armstrong Gibbs

26   CHI VUOL LA ZINGARELLA   Giovanni Paisiello

34   CHRISTOPHER ROBIN IS SAYING HIS PRAYERS   H. Fraser-Simson

31   CLOUD-SHADOWS   James H. Rogers

38   CRABBED AGE AND YOUTH   Maude Valérie White

42   CRUCIFIXION   arranged by John Payne

48   EL MAJO TIMIDO (The Timid Majo)   Enrique Granados

45   EVENSONG   Liza Lehmann

50   GO 'WAY FROM MY WINDOW   John Jacob Niles

52   ICI-BAS! (Here Below)   Gabriel Fauré

58   JESUS WALKED THIS LONESOME VALLEY   arranged by Gordon Myers

55   THE LAMB   Theodore Chanler

62   THE LASS FROM THE LOW COUNTREE   John Jacob Niles

66   THE LORD IS MY SHEPHERD   Peter Tchaikovsky

76   LOVELIEST OF TREES   John Duke

82   MORNING   Oley Speaks

94   O REST IN THE LORD   Felix Mendelssohn

97   OH SLEEP, WHY DOST THOU LEAVE ME?   George Frideric Handel

100   OPEN OUR EYES   Will C. Macfarlane

86   PRAYER   David W. Guion

90   PREGÚNTALE A LAS ESTRELLAS   arranged by Edward Kilenyi

71   SILENT NOON   Ralph Vaughan Williams

105   DER SCHWUR (The Vow)   Erik Meyer-Helmund

108   THE SKY ABOVE THE ROOF   Ralph Vaughan Williams

112   THE STATUE AT CZARSKOE-SELO   César Cui

126   THIS LITTLE ROSE   William Roy

120   TURN THEN THINE EYES   Henry Purcell

114   VOLKSLIEDCHEN (In the Garden)   Robert Schumann

116   WIE MELODIEN (A Thought Like Music)   Johannes Brahms

123   WIND OF THE WESTERN SEA   Graham Peel

AMERICAN LULLABY

words and music by
Gladys Rich

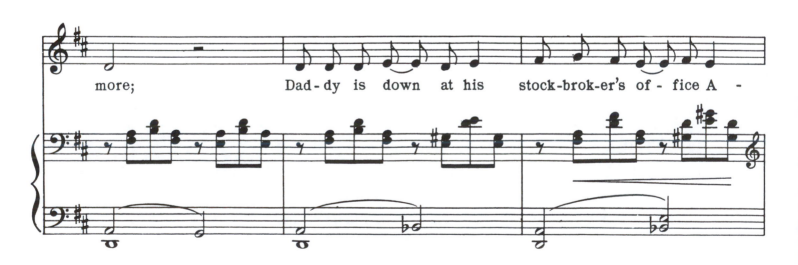

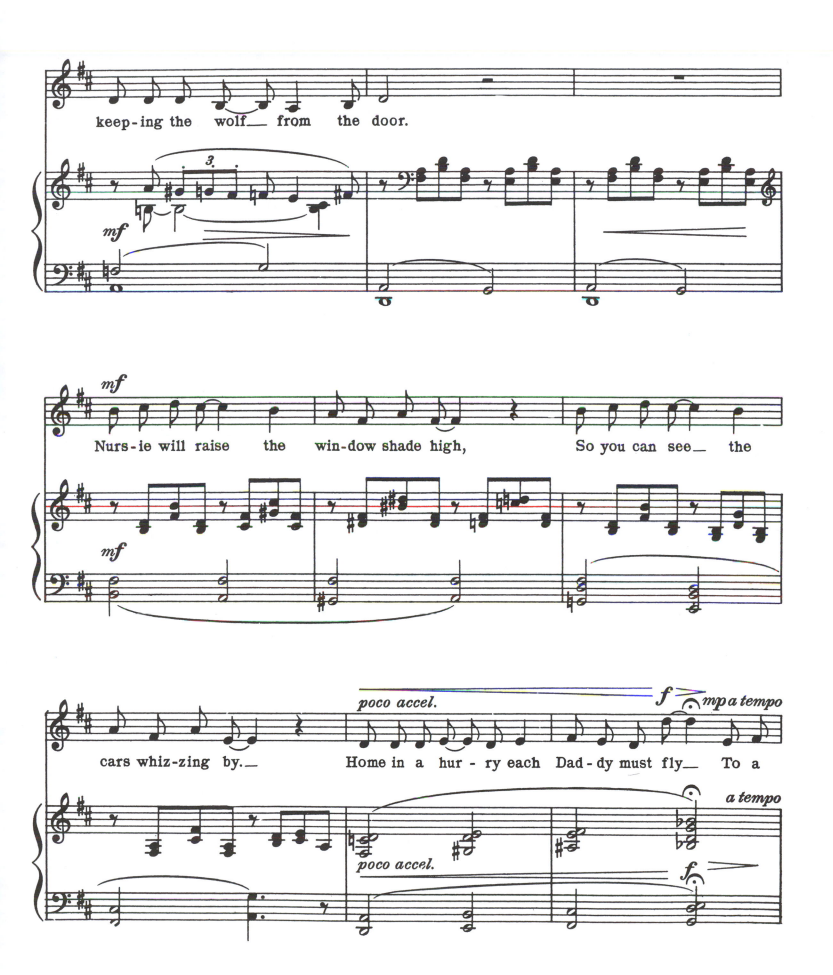

ba - by like you.

Hush - a - bye, you sweet lit - tle ba - by, And

close those pret - ty blue eyes. Moth - er has gone to her

week - ly bridge par - ty To get her wee ba - by the prize.

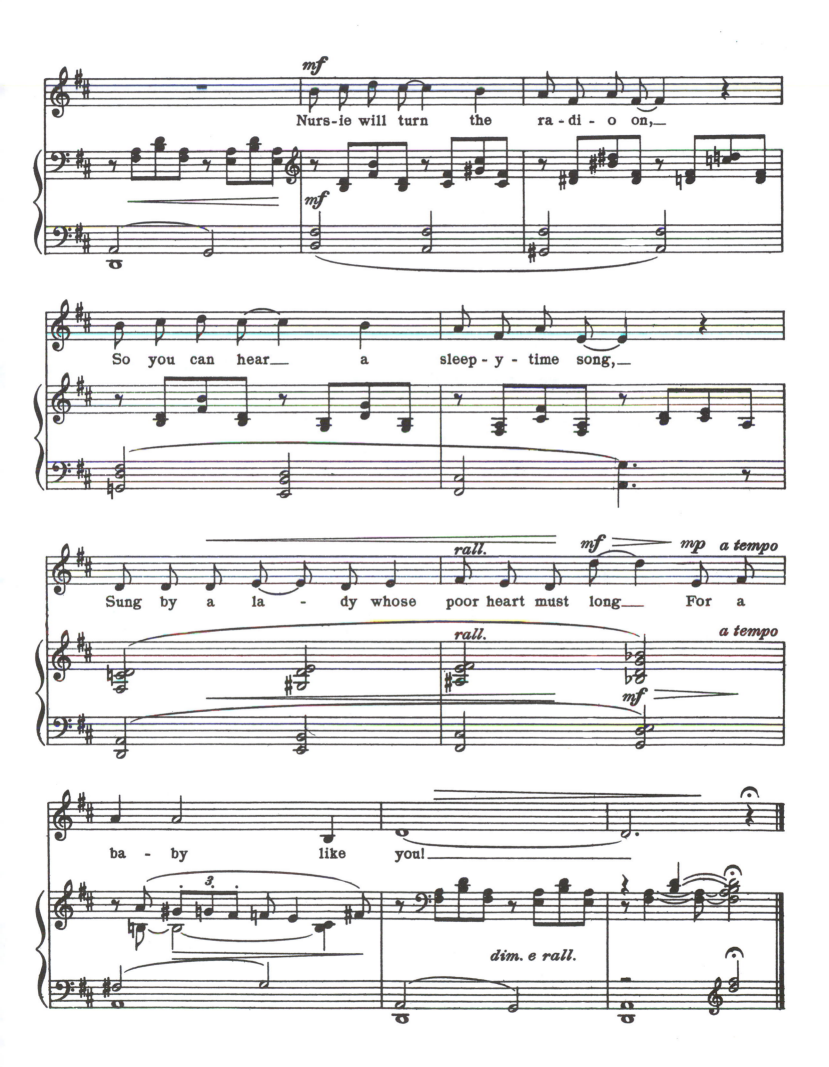

Nurs-ie will turn the ra-di-o on,__

So you can hear__ a sleep-y-time song,__

Sung by a la - dy whose poor heart must long__ For a

ba - by like you!__

L'ANNEAU D'ARGENT
(The Silver Ring)

Cécile Chaminade

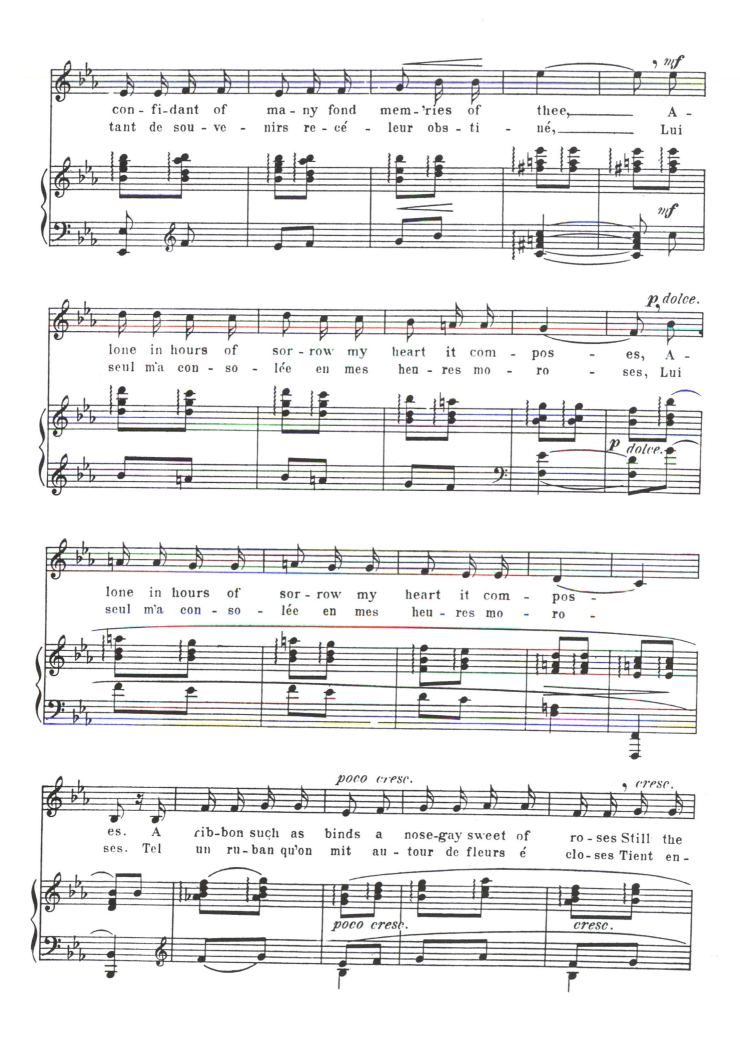

home, that nev-er-more mine eye shall see,   When
cueil, de blanc sa-tin ca-pi-ton-né,   Lors-

poco rit. dolciss   *a tempo.* *mf*

I shall lie a-sleep all pale a-mid the ros - es, I
que je dor-mi - rai, très pâ - le sur des ro - ses, Je

*poco rit. **ppp** dolciss.* *m.g.* *a tempo. mf*

Led. *⁕*

, p

will that on my with-er-ing fin-ger there be The sil-ver ring so
veux qu'il brille en - cor à mon doigt dé-char - né, Le cher an-neau d'ar-

p

rr

dear that once thou gav-est me.
gent que vous m'a-vez don - né.

m.g.

pp

Led.

DIE BEKEHRTE
(The Converted One)

Johann Wolfgang von Goethe

Max Stange

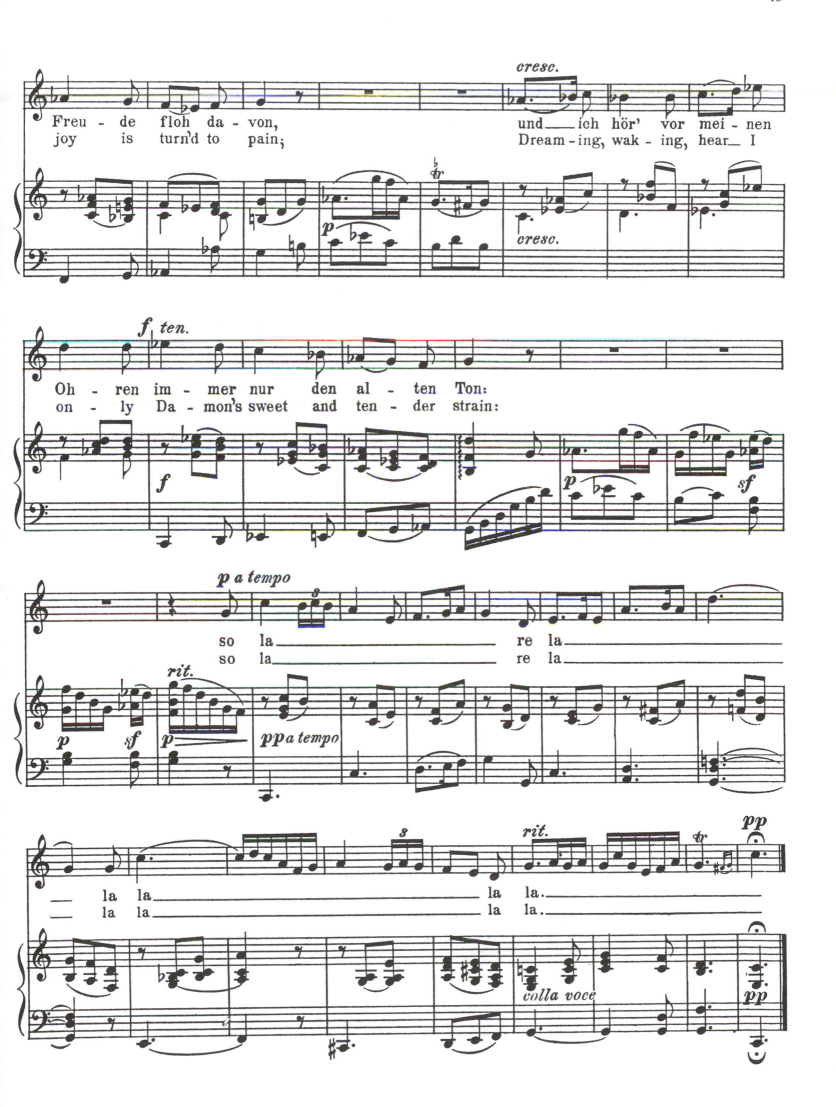

Freu - de floh da - von, und ich hör' vor mei - nen
joy is turn'd to pain; Dream - ing, wak - ing, hear I

Oh - ren im - mer nur den al - ten Ton:
on - ly Da - mon's sweet and ten - der strain:

so la_____ re la_____
so la_____ re la_____

la la_____ la la._____
la la_____ la la._____

DER BLUMENSTRAUSS
(The Nosegay)

Felix Mendelssohn

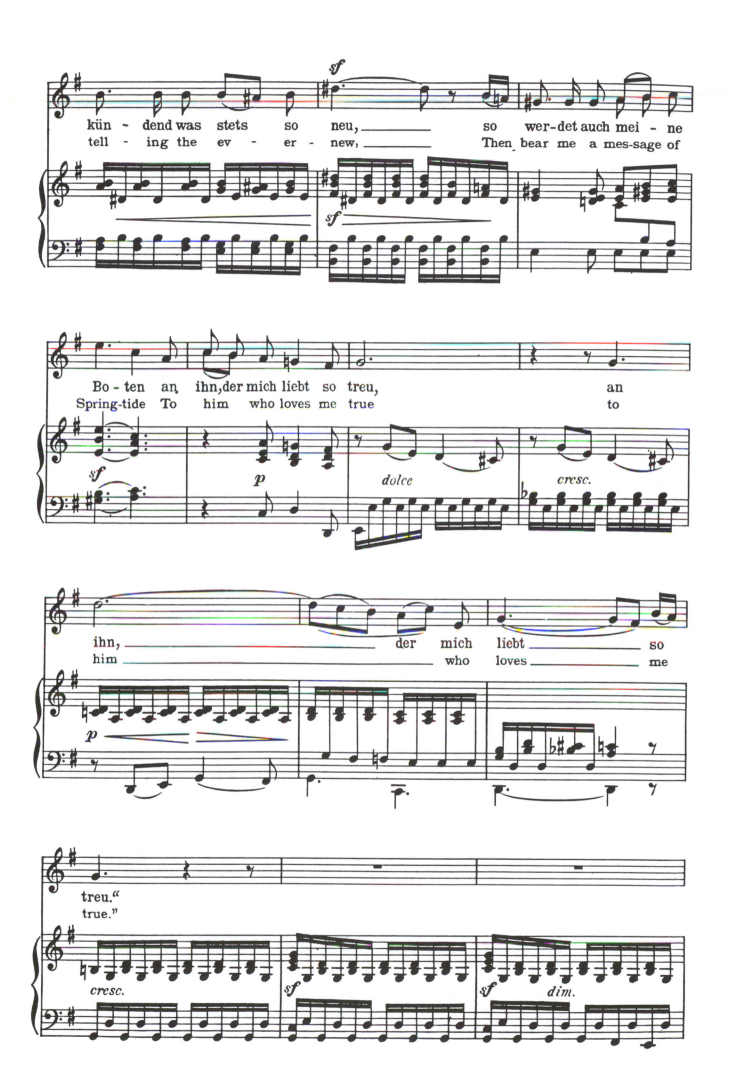

kün - dend was stets so neu, _____ so wer-det auch mei - ne
tell - ing the ev - er - new, _____ Then bear me a mes-sage of

Bo - ten an ihn, der mich liebt so treu, an
Spring-tide To him who loves me true to

ihn, _____ der mich liebt _____ so
him _____ who loves _____ me

treu."
true."

So ü - ber-schaut sie die
Light - ly the flow - ers en -

Ha - - be und ord - net den lieb - li - chen Strauss, _____ und
twin - - ing, How deft - ly her fin - gers toil: _____ She

reicht dem Freunde die Ga - - be, und weicht sei-nem Bli - cke aus. Was
hands them to one__ who nears her, A - void - ing his gaze the while. What

Blu - men und Far - ben mei - nen, o deu - tet, o fragt das
flow - ers and hues be - to - ken, Di - vine it, oh, ask__ it

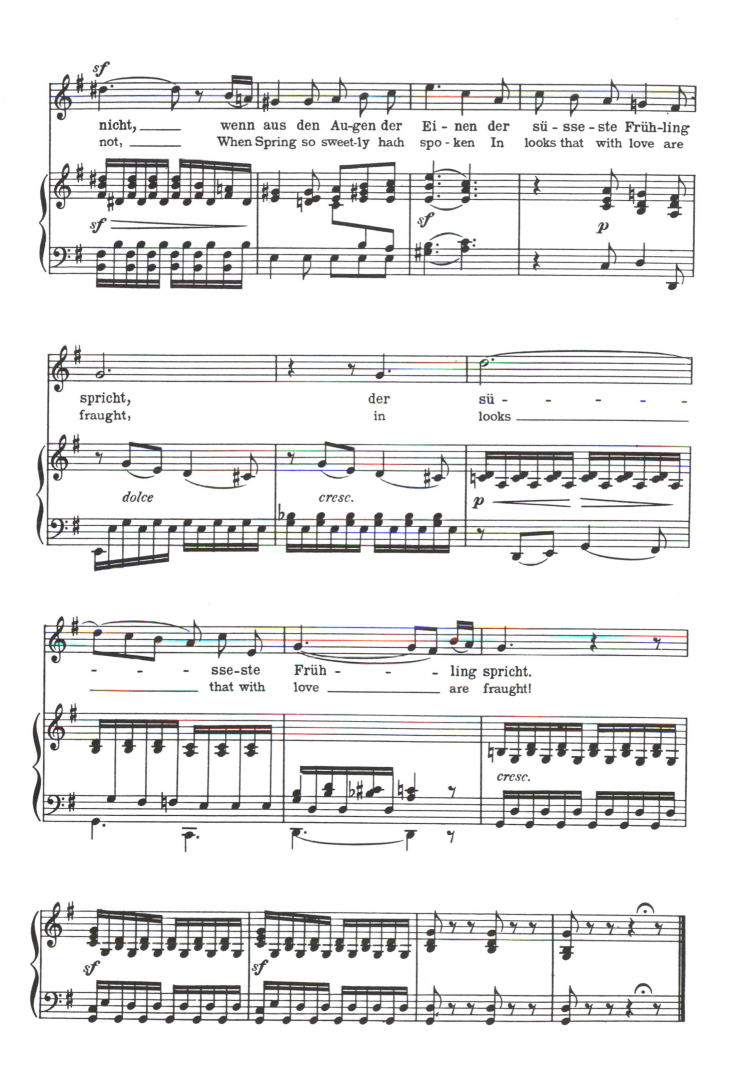

THE CHERRY TREE

Margaret Rose

Armstrong Gibbs

Time of performance 2 –2¼ mins.

Sing, birds! Sing songs of the

Spring - time, Sing high ____

____ on the cher - ry tree. ____

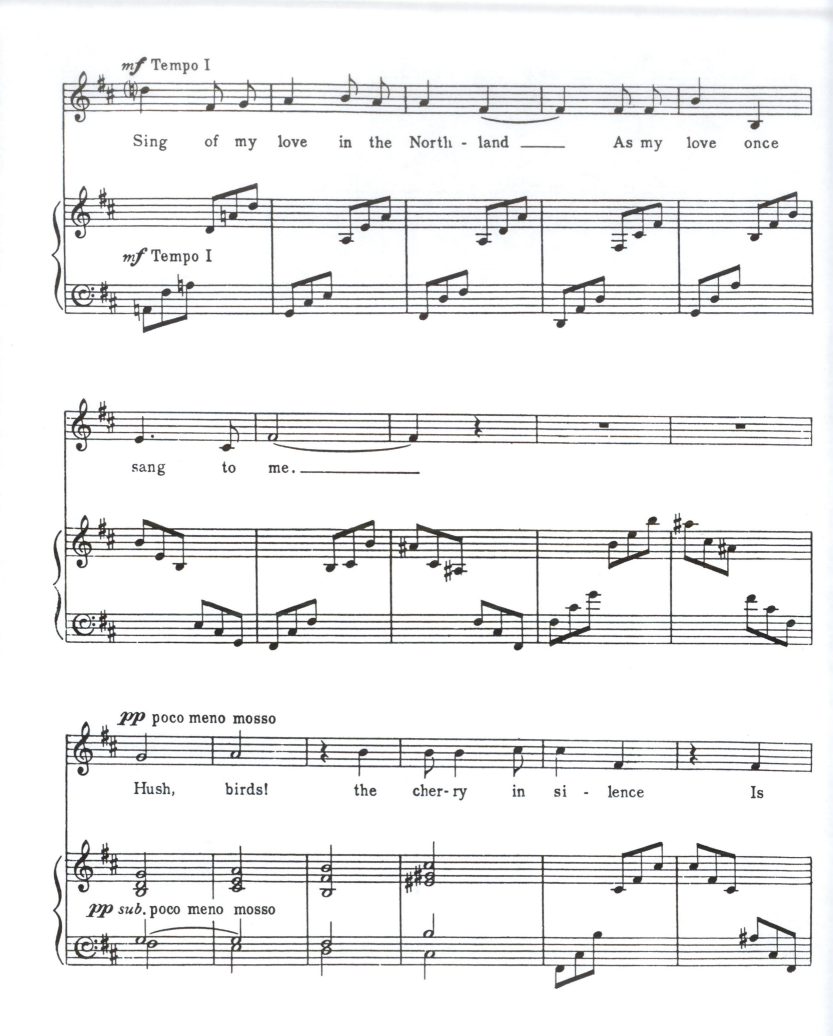

Sing of my love in the North - land ____ As my love once

sang to me. _____

Hush, birds! the cher-ry in si - lence Is

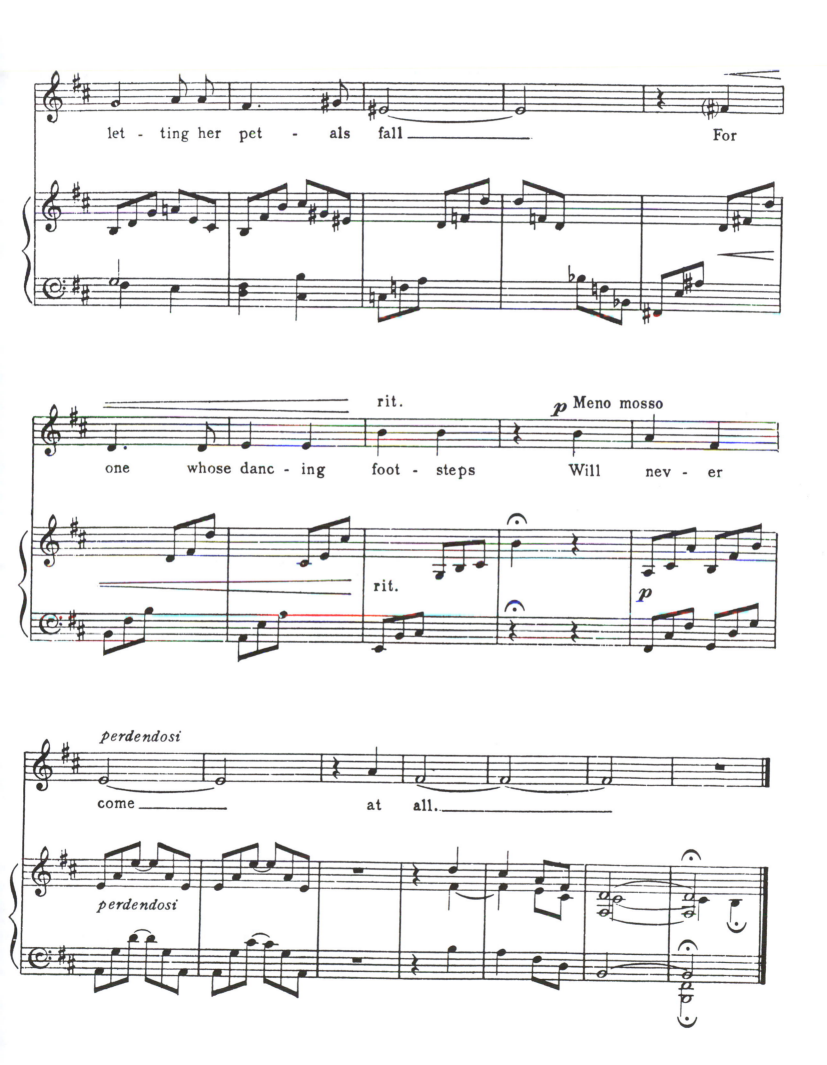

CHI VUOL LA ZINGARELLA

Giovanni Paisiello

Chi vuol la zin-ga-
Who'll try the Gip-sy

rel-la gra - ziosa.ac-corta e bel-la? Si - gnori,ec-co-la__ qua, si-
pretty, So winning,wise and wit-ty, As__ one and all may see, As

gnori,ec - co-la qua. Le don-ne sul bal - co - ne
one and all may see? For la-dies at their win - dow

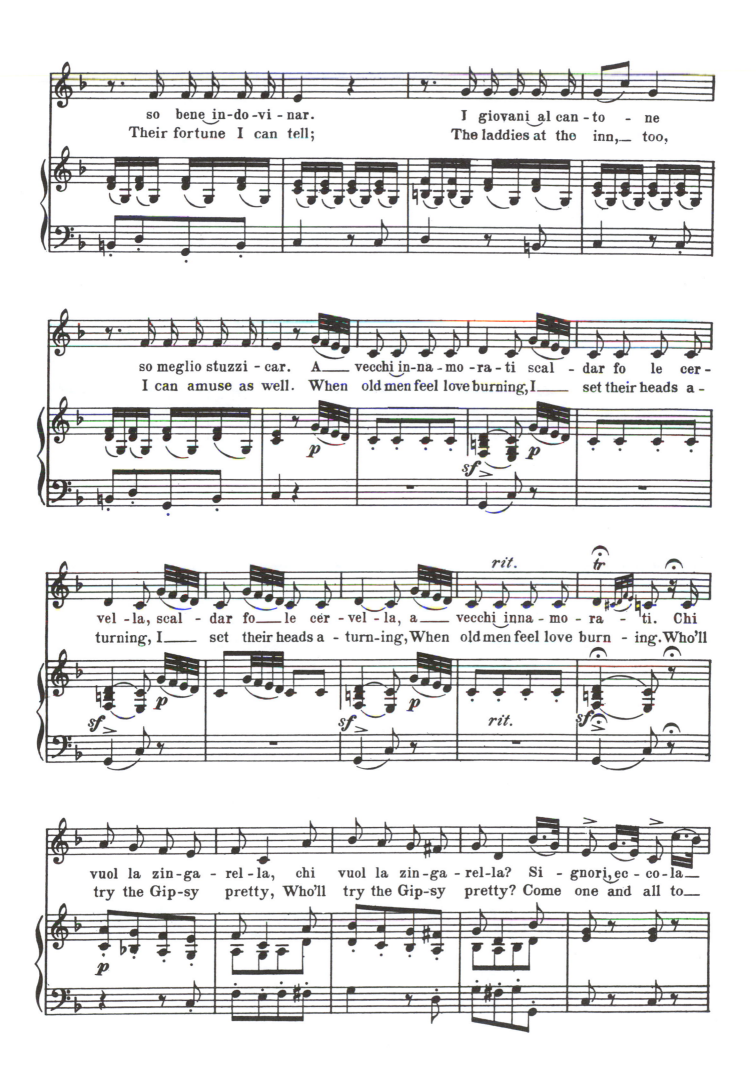

so bene in-do-vi-nar.
Their fortune I can tell;

I giovani al can-to-ne
The laddies at the inn,— too,

so meglio stuzzi-car. A—— vecchi in-na-mo-ra-ti scal-dar fo le cer-
I can amuse as well. When old men feel love burning, I—— set their heads a-

vel-la, scal-dar fo—— le cer-vel-la, a—— vecchi inna-mo-ra-ti. Chi
turning, I—— set their heads a-turn-ing, When old men feel love burn-ing. Who'll

vuol la zin-ga-rel-la, chi vuol la zin-ga-rel-la? Si-gnori, ec-co-la——
try the Gip-sy pretty, Who'll try the Gip-sy pretty? Come one and all to——

CLOUD-SHADOWS

Katharine Pyle

James H. Rogers

Slowly and dreamily

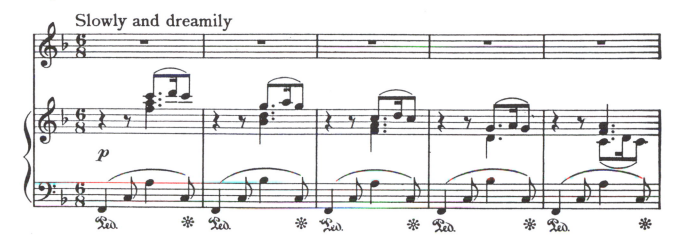

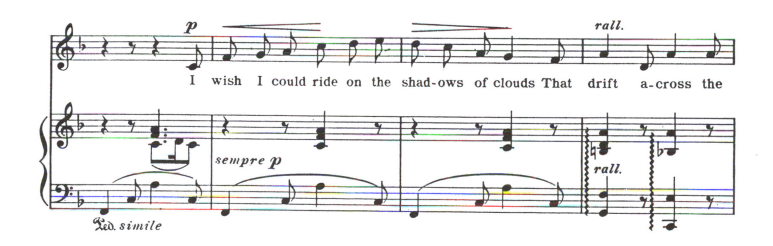

I wish I could ride on the shad-ows of clouds That drift a-cross the

hill; O-ver the mead-ow and out of sight They sweep so smooth and still.

O - ver the dai - sy field they passed, And not a dai - sy stirr'd; They

moved like char - i - ots grand and slow, But nev - er a sound was heard.

CHRISTOPHER ROBIN IS SAYING HIS PRAYERS
(Vespers)

A. A. Milne

H. Fraser-Simson

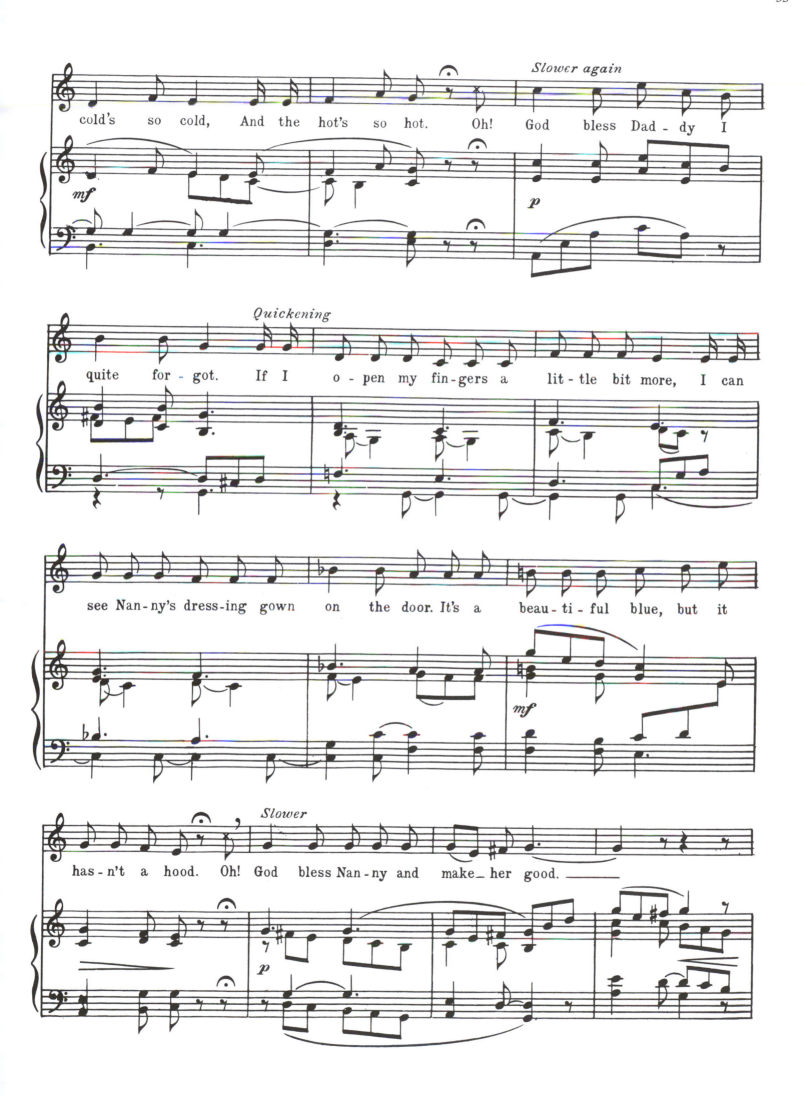

36

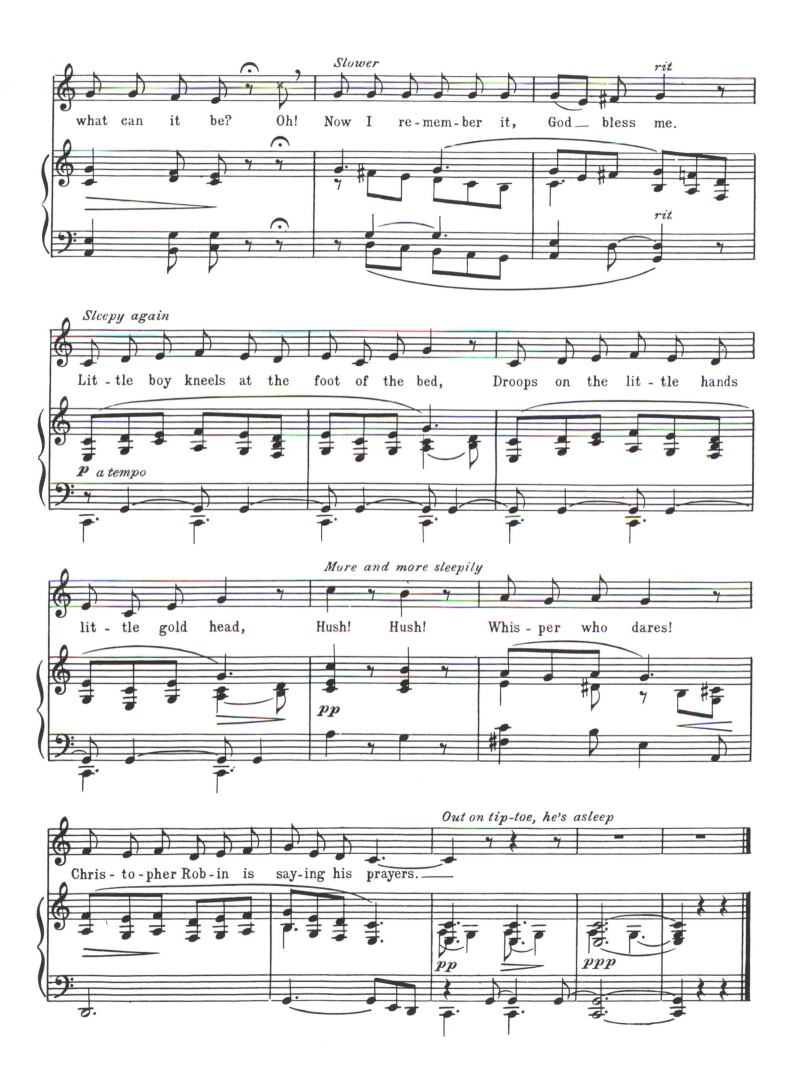

CRABBED AGE AND YOUTH

William Shakespeare

Maude Valérie White

Allegro con brio.

Attácca súbito
Con brio.

f ma leggiero

Crab - bed Age and Youth Can - not live.... to - ge - ther;

f ma leggiero

Youth is full... of plea - sure, Age is full of care.

Con spirito.

Youth like sum-mer morn,.... Age.. like win-ter wea-ther,

Youth................. like sum - mer brave, Age... like win - ter

bare.

Youth is full of plea - sure, Age is full of care;

Youth is full of sport, Age's breath is short;

ff con fuoco

molto rit.

40

I do a - dore thee; Oh! my love, my

love is young! Age, I do de - fy thee,

rit - ard - an - do

Age, I do de - fy thee! O sweet shep - herd,

Largo

hie thee! For me - thinks thou

a tempo

stay'st too long.

rit.

colla voce *ff a tempo*

CRUCIFIXION

African American spiritual
arranged by John Payne

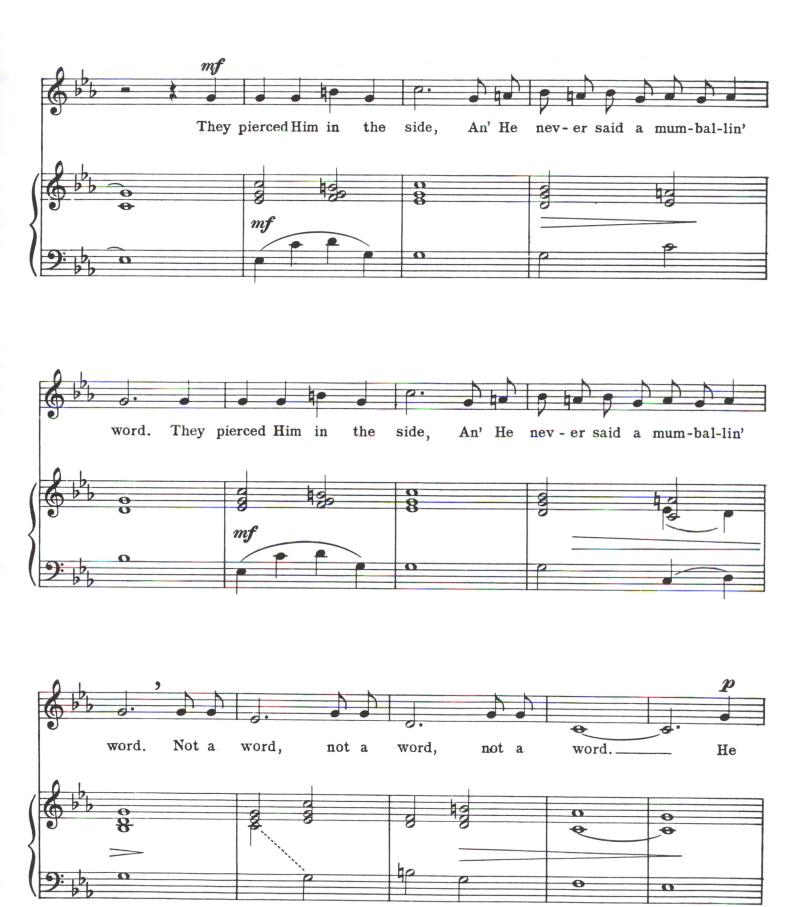

They pierced Him in the side, An' He nev-er said a mum-bal-lin' word. They pierced Him in the side, An' He nev-er said a mum-bal-lin' word. Not a word, not a word, not a word._____ He

EVENSONG

Constance Morgan

Liza Lehmann

Fold your white wings, dear An - - gels,

Fold your white wings;

Dew falls and the night - in - gale Soft - -

EL MAJO TIMIDO
(The Timid Majo)

Llega a mi reja y me mira por la noche un majo.
Que en cuanto me ve y suspira se va calle abajo.
¡Ah! Que tío mas tardío,
Si asi se pasa la vida,
Estoy divertida.

At night, under my window, a majo* comes to look at me.
After he sees me, he sighs and goes on his way.
Ah! What a dull man.
If this is how it's going to be,
Some fun I'll have!

* majo is an untranslatable word for a dashing, handsome lover

Enrique Granados

pi - ra se va ca - lle a - ba - jo

¡Ay que ti - o mas tar - di - o

Sia - si se pa - sa la vi - da es - toy di - ver - ti - da

GO 'WAY FROM MY WINDOW

words and music by
John Jacob Niles

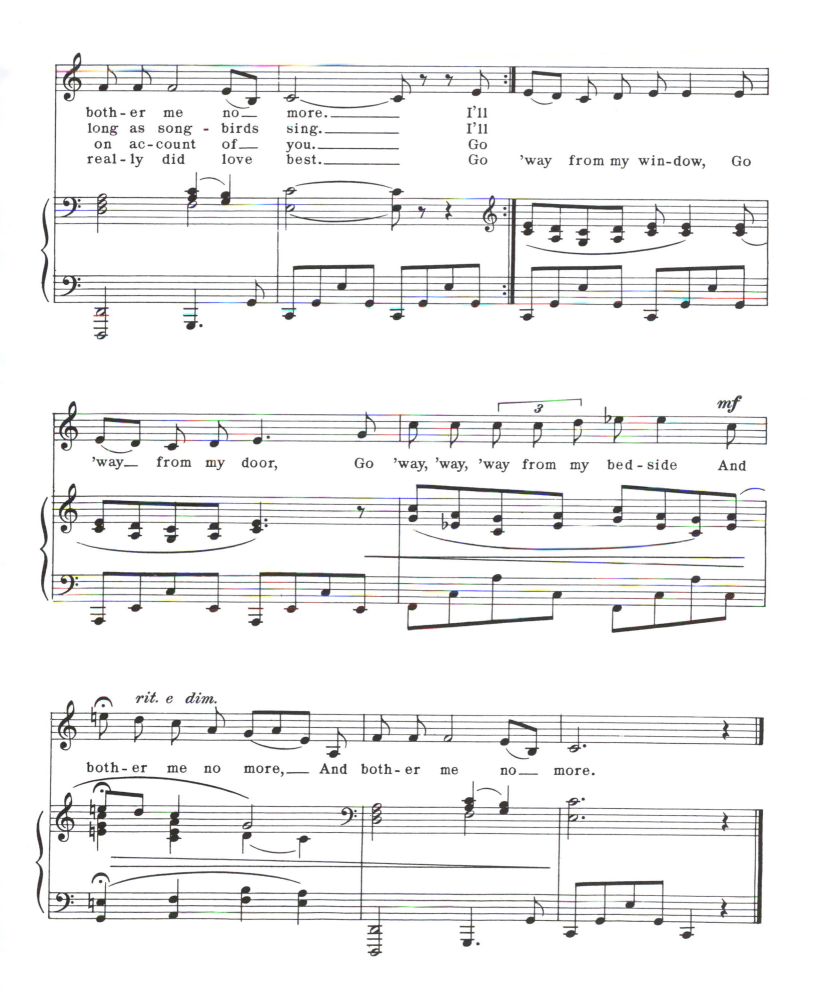

ICI-BAS!
(Here Below)

Sully Prudhomme

Gabriel Fauré

To be sung in parlando style

THE LAMB

William Blake

Theodore Chanler

Gave thee such a ten - der voice, Mak - ing all the vales re - joice?

p dolce

rit

a tempo, semplice

Lit - tle Lamb, who made thee? Dost thou know who made thee?

a tempo
semplice

rit

a tempo

a tempo

poco rit

𝆏 a tempo

Lit - tle Lamb, I'll tell thee, Lit - tle Lamb, I'll tell thee:

a tempo

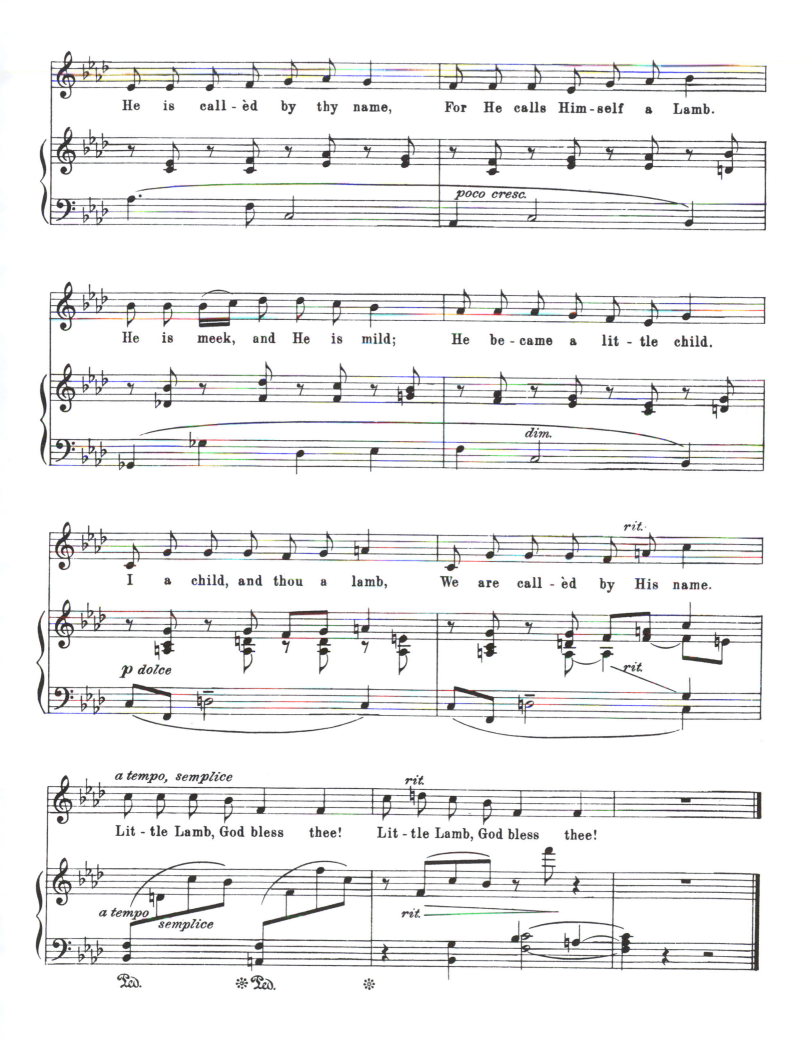

JESUS WALKED THIS LONESOME VALLEY

arranged by Gordon Myers

Andante

1. Je - sus walked this lone-some val - ley, He had to

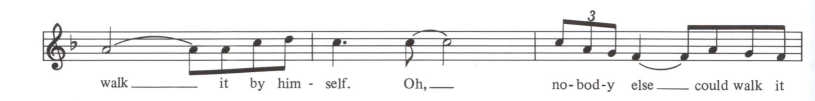

walk it by him - self. Oh, no-bod-y else could walk it

for him, He had to walk it by him - self. 2. We must

walk this lone-some val - ley, we have to walk it by our-

selves.   Oh,____   no-bod-y else ____ can walk it

cresc.   *mf*   *decresc.*

for   us,   we have to walk   it   by____   our-

p

selves.   3. We must clasp_____ our hands to-

mp

geth-er,   we have to clasp_____ them in the air.   Oh, __

cresc.   *mf*

no-bod-y else can clasp them for us, we have to

clasp them by our-selves. 4. We must

lift our hearts to heav-en, we have to

lift them up our-selves. Oh, no-bod-y else can lift them

for us, the prayer of broth - er - hood___ is there. 5. Je - sus

walked_____ this lone-some val-ley, He had to walk_____ it by him-

self. Oh,___ no-bod-y else_____ could walk it for him, He had to

walk it by___ him - self._____

Note: To dramatize 'loneliness', the last two measures
of the accompaniment may be omitted.

THE LASS FROM THE LOW COUNTREE

John Jacob Niles

Oh, he was a lord of high de-gree, And she was a lass from the Low Coun-tree, But she loved his lord-ship so ten-der-ly! Oh, sor-row, sing

sor - row! Now she sleeps in the val - ley where the wild - flow - ers nod, And

no one knows she loved him but her - self and God.___ One

morn, when the sun was on the mead, He passed by her door on a

64

THE LORD IS MY SHEPHERD

Peter Tchaikovsky
adapted and arranged by
Richard Maxwell and
Fred Feibel

Psalm 23

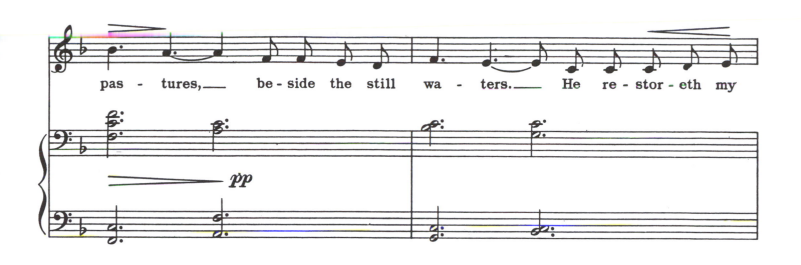

pas - tures,___ be - side the still wa - ters.___ He re - stor - eth my

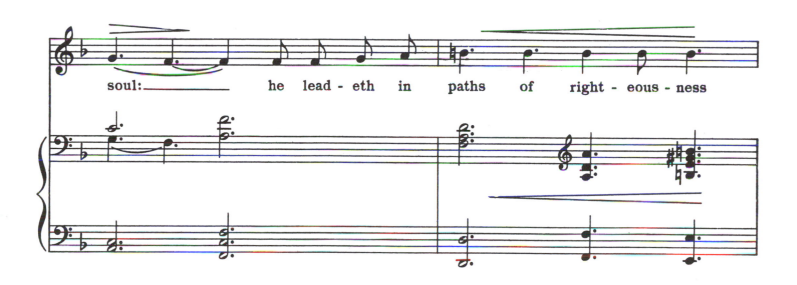

soul:___ he lead - eth in paths of right - eous - ness

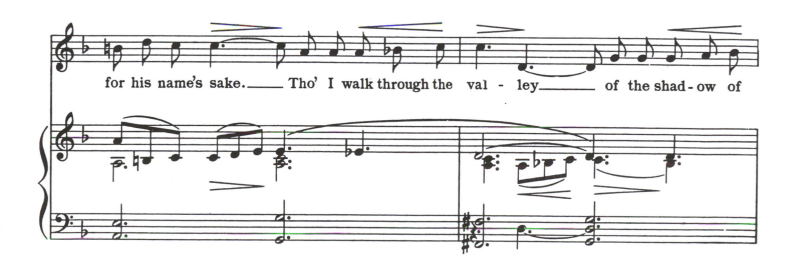

for his name's sake.___ Tho' I walk through the val - ley___ of the shad - ow of

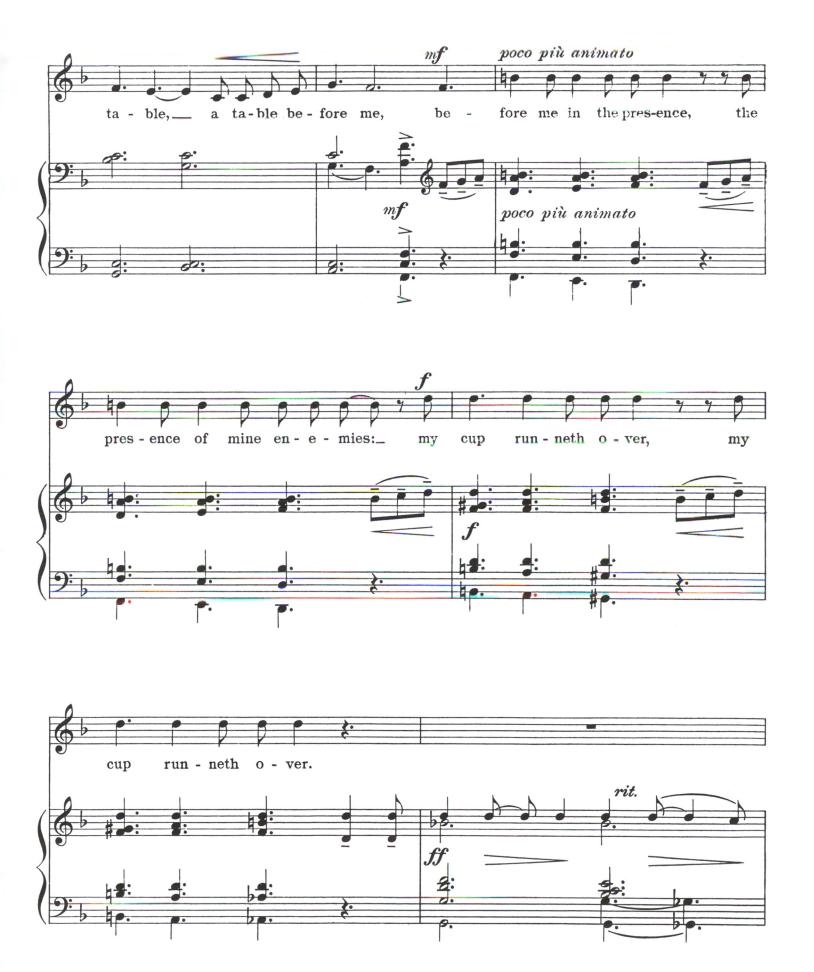

SILENT NOON

Dante Gabriel Rossetti

Ralph Vaughan Williams

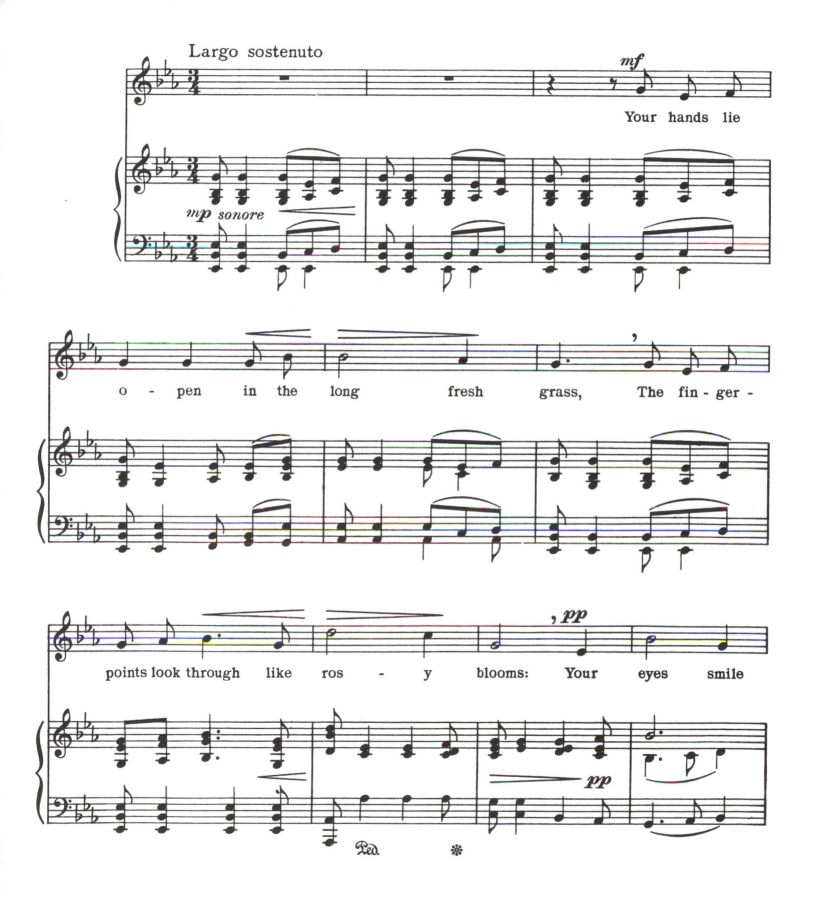

peace. The pas-ture gleams and glooms 'Neath bil - low-ing

mf

cresc.

skies that scat-ter and a - mass.

f

Poco più mosso

pp

p

All round our nest, far as the eye can pass, Are

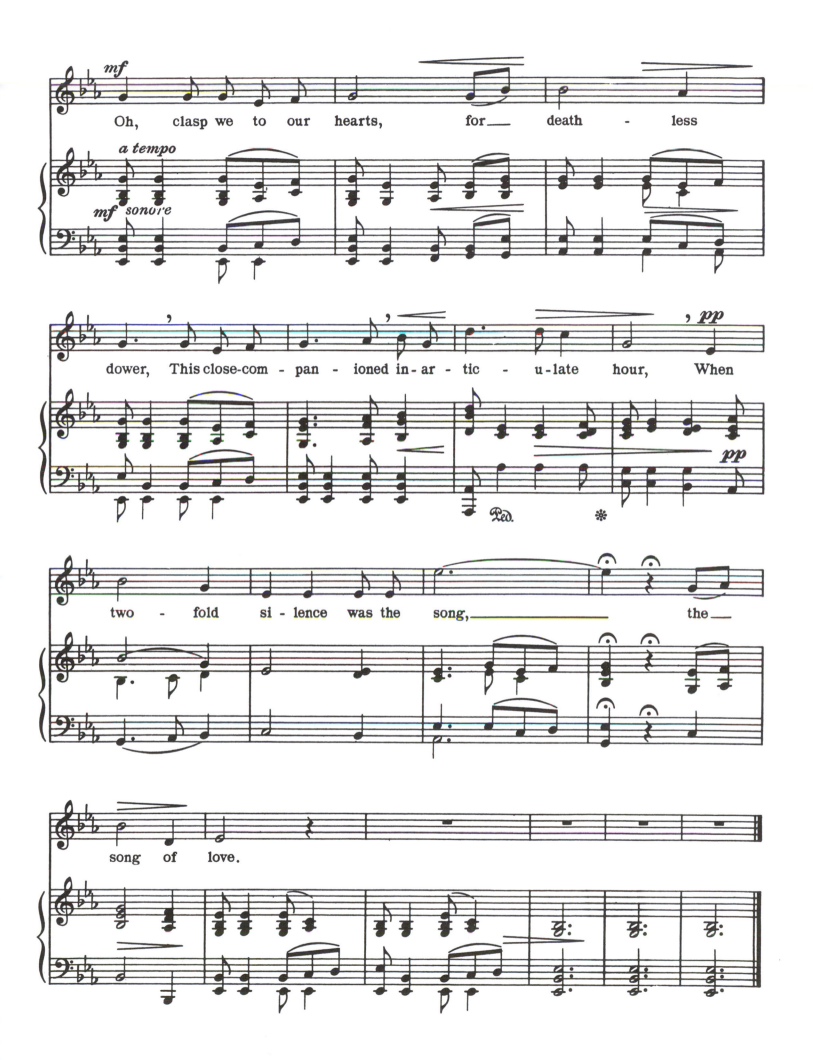

LOVELIEST OF TREES

A.E. Housman*

John Duke

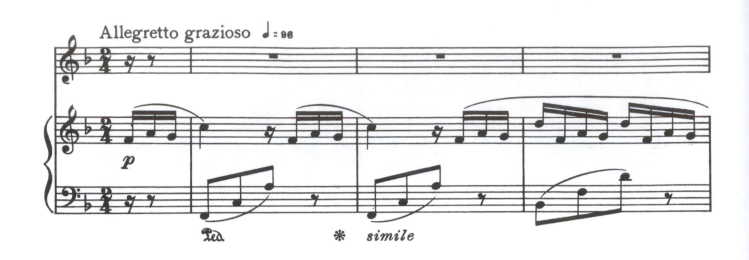

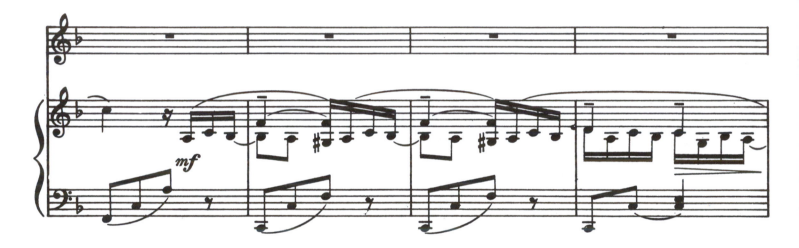

*Poem from "A Shropshire Lad." Printed by permission of Grant Richards, London, publisher.

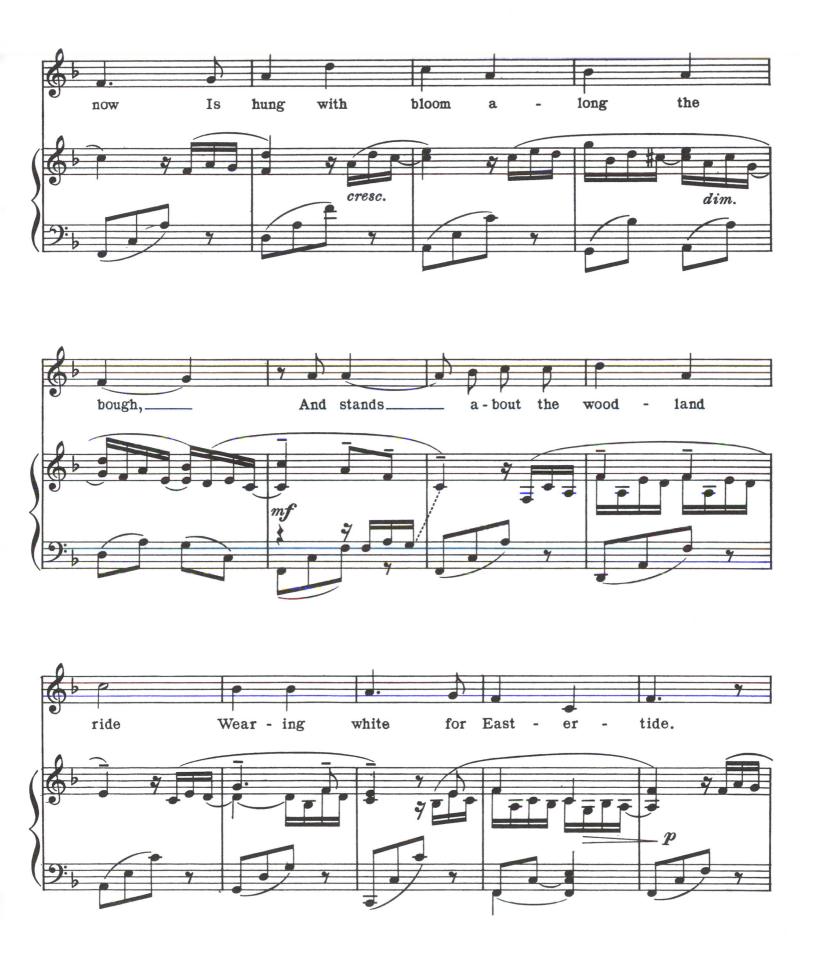

now Is hung with bloom a - long the bough,_____ And stands_____ a - bout the wood - land ride Wear - ing white for East - er - tide.

Now, of my three - score years and ten,

Twen - ty will not come a - gain,

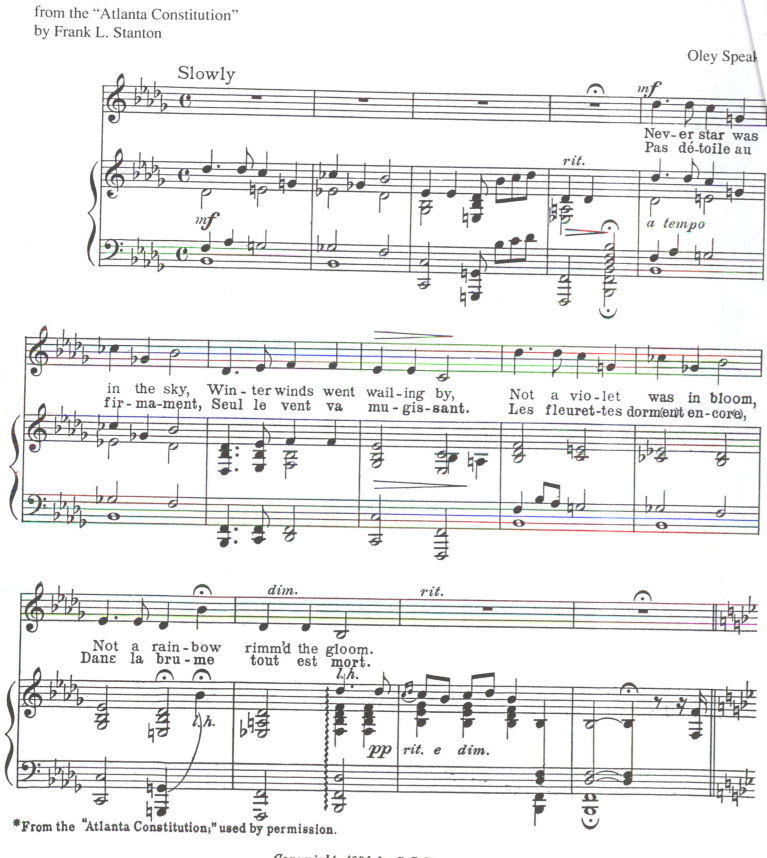

MORNING

from the "Atlanta Constitution"
by Frank L. Stanton

Oley Speak

Slowly

Nev - er star was
Pas dé - toile au

in the sky, Win - ter winds went wail - ing by, Not a vio - let was in bloom,
fir - ma - ment, Seul le vent va mu - gis - sant. Les fleuret - tes dorment en - core,

Not a rain - bow rimm'd the gloom.
Dans la bru - me tout est mort.

*From the "Atlanta Constitution;" used by permission.

Copyright, 1931, by G. Schirmer, Inc.

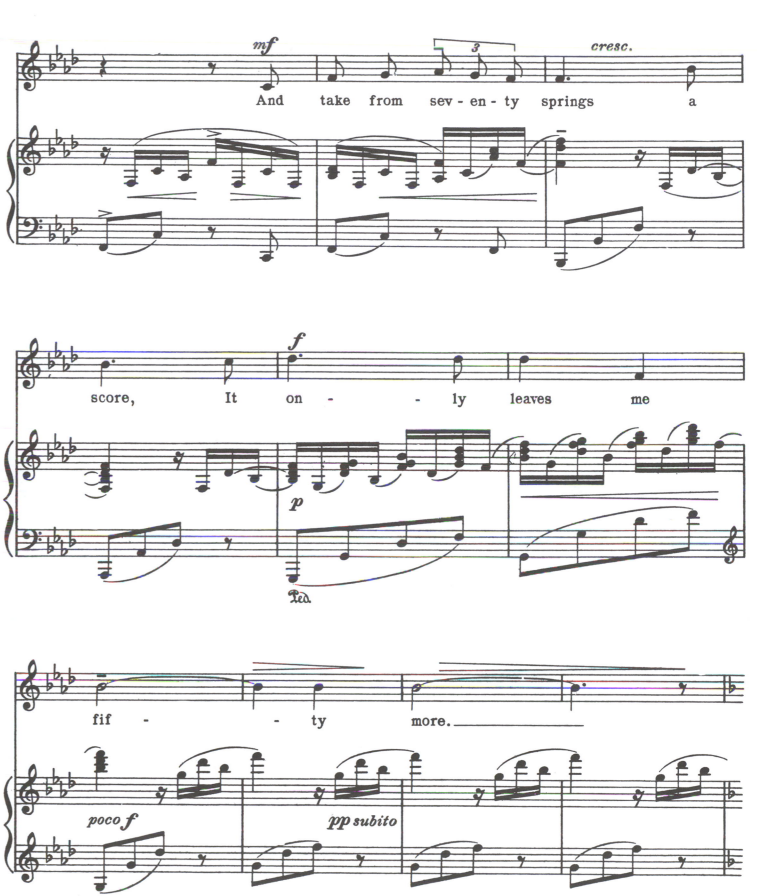

And take from sev - en - ty springs a

score, It on - ly leaves me

fif - ty more.

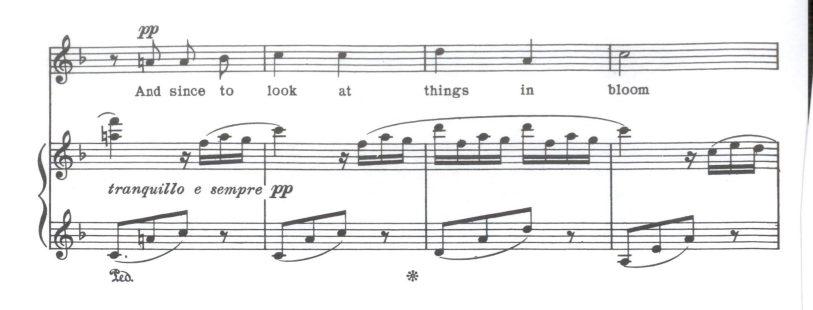

84

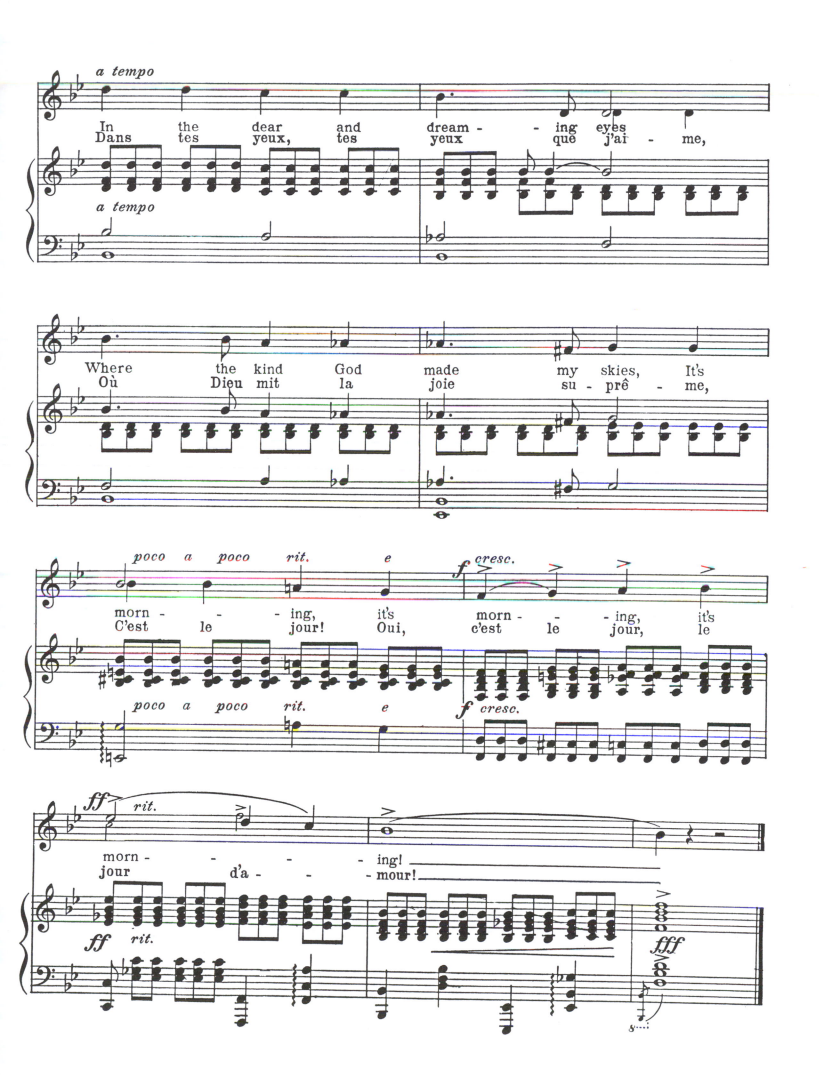

PRAYER

Hermann Hagedorn

David W. Guion

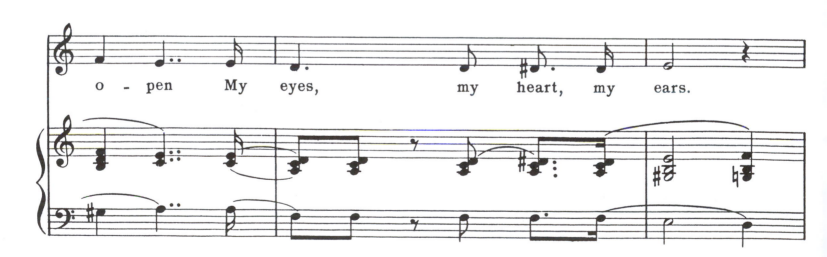

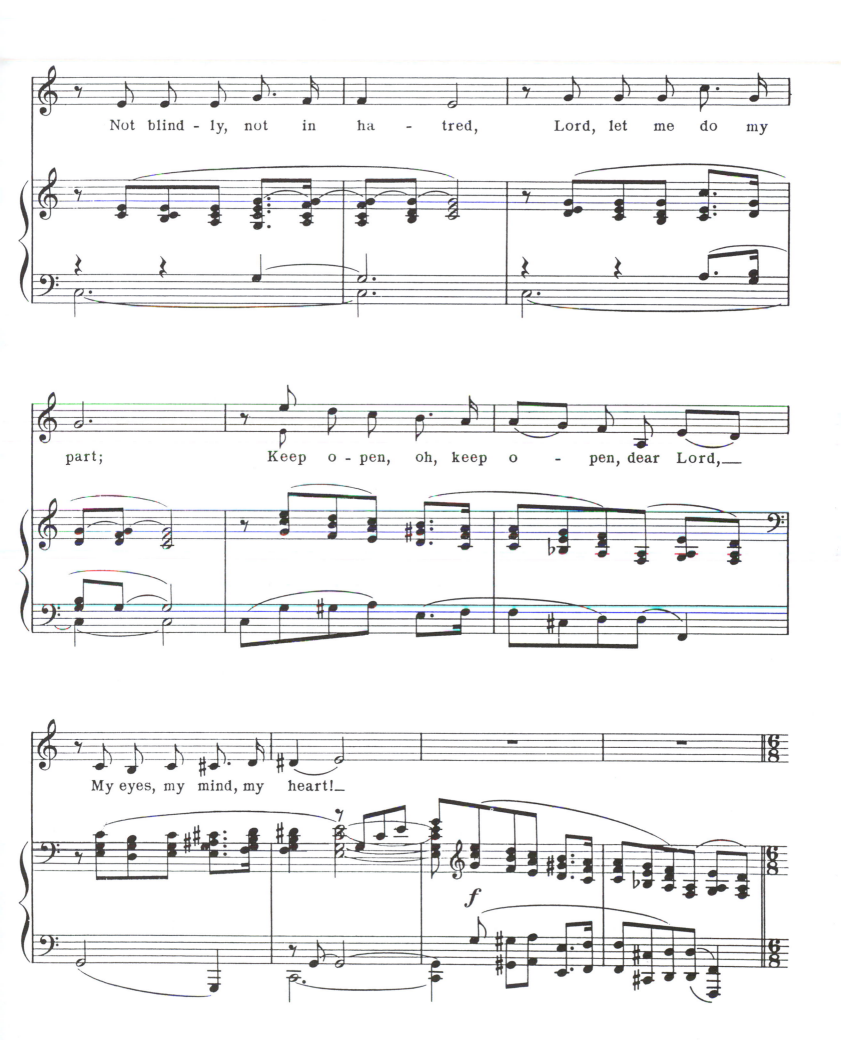

Not blind - ly, not in ha - tred, Lord, let me do my

part;

Keep o - pen, oh, keep o - pen, dear Lord,___

My eyes, my mind, my heart!___

f

God,   Hear Thou my plead - ing, Hear Thou   my prayer.

Lord, in   this hour   of   tu - mult,   Lord in this night of   fears,___

Keep o - pen, oh, keep o - pen   My eyes,   my   ears.

PREGÚNTALE A LAS ESTRELLAS

Latin American folksong
arranged by Edward Kilenyi

O REST IN THE LORD
from *Elijah*

Psalm 37

Felix Mendelssohn

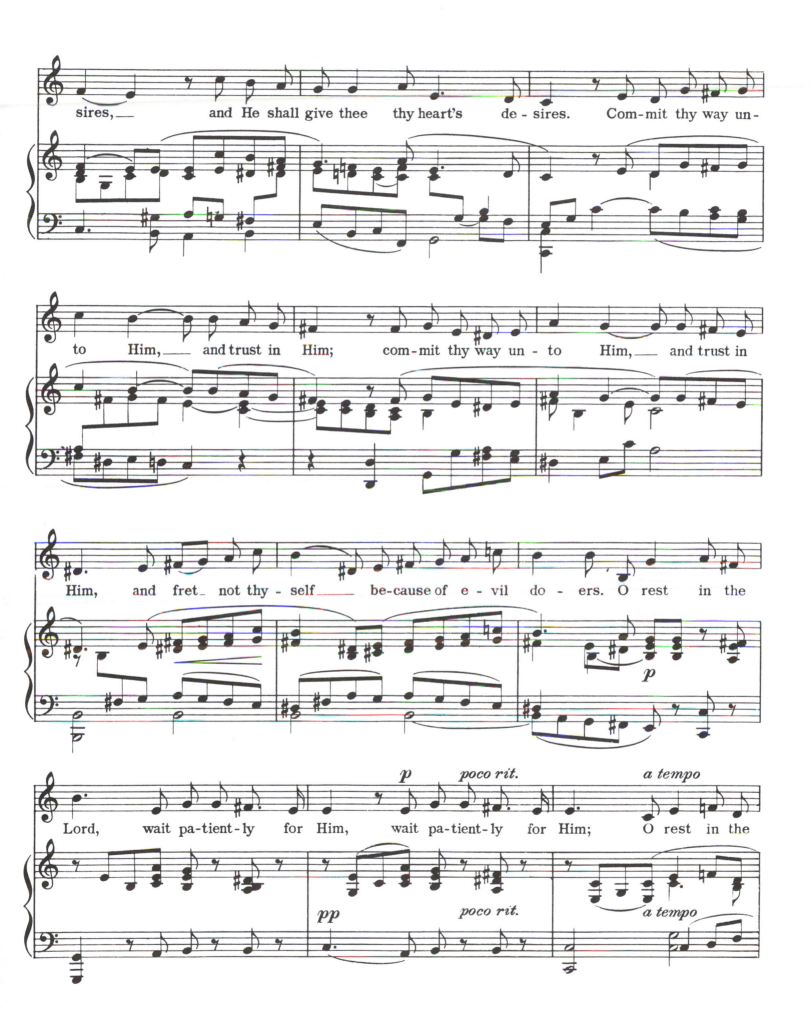

OH SLEEP, WHY DOST THOU LEAVE ME?

from *Semele*

William Congreve

George Frideric Handel

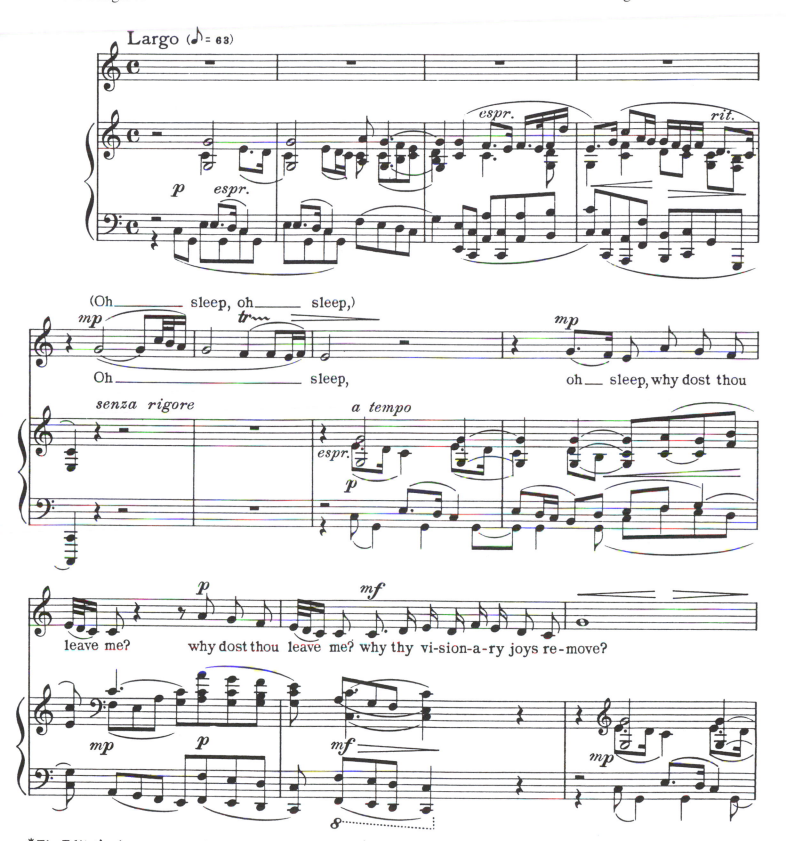

*The Editor's piano accompaniment is founded on Handel's unfigured bass.

98

OPEN OUR EYES

Frederic West MacDonald

Will C. Macfarlane

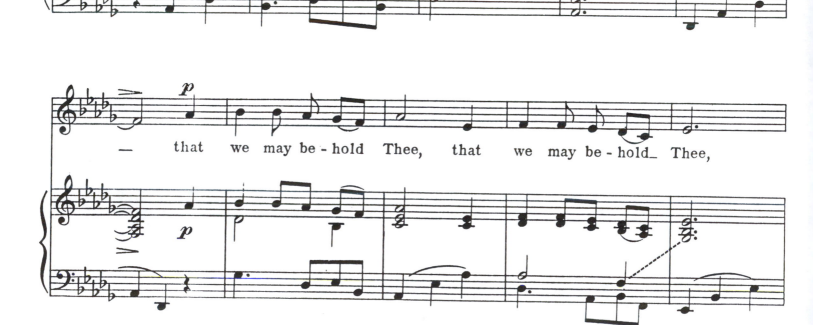

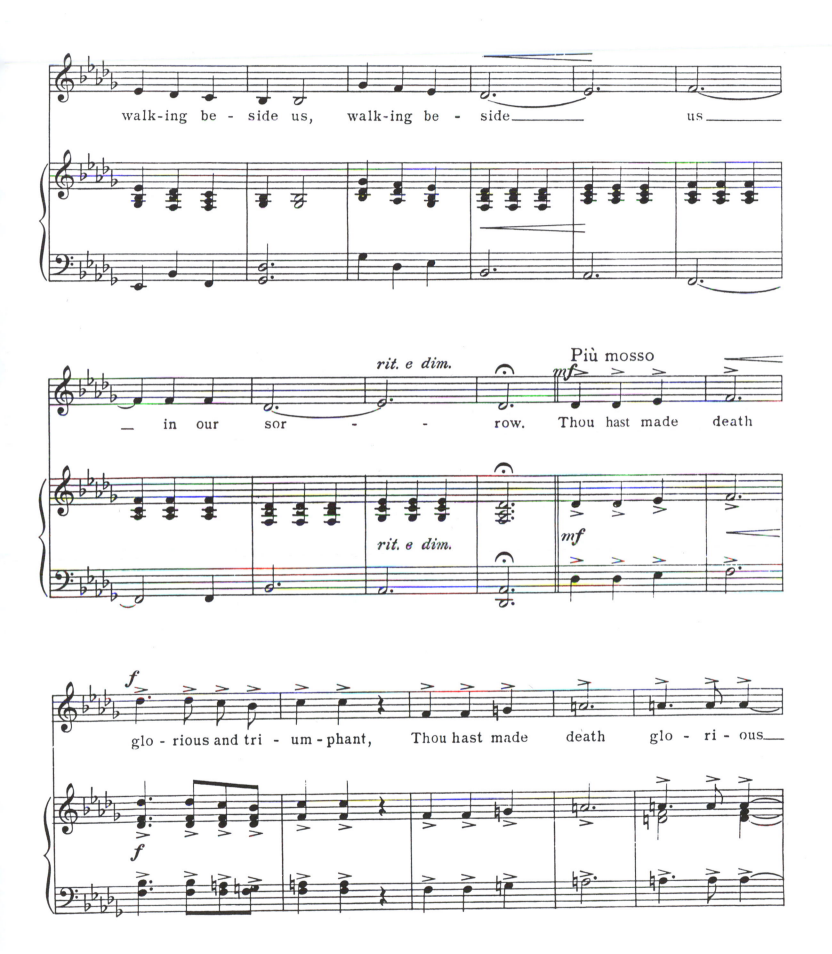

and tri - um - phant;

Tempo I°

For through its

por - tals we en - ter in - to the pres - ence of the Liv - ing

God, in - to the pres - ence of the Liv - ing God;

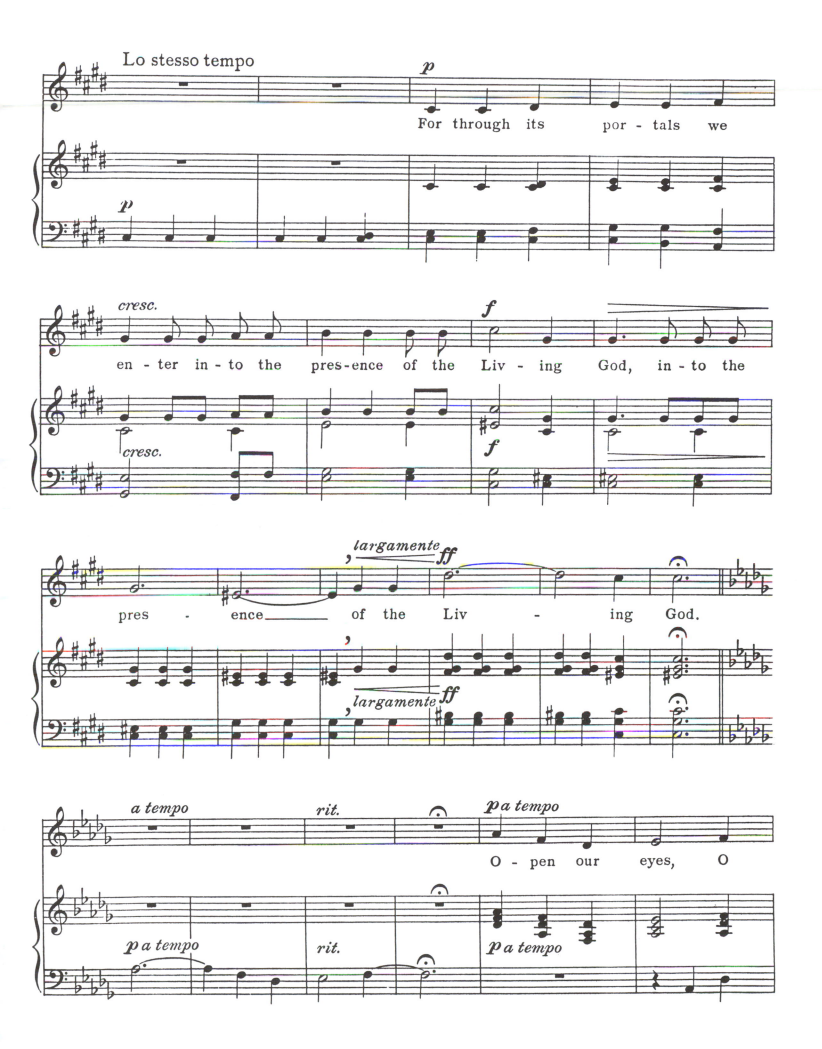

For through its por - tals we en - ter in - to the pres - ence of the Liv - ing God, in - to the pres - ence___ of the Liv - ing God.

O - pen our eyes, O

104

DER SCHWUR
(The Vow)

Erik Meyer-Helmund

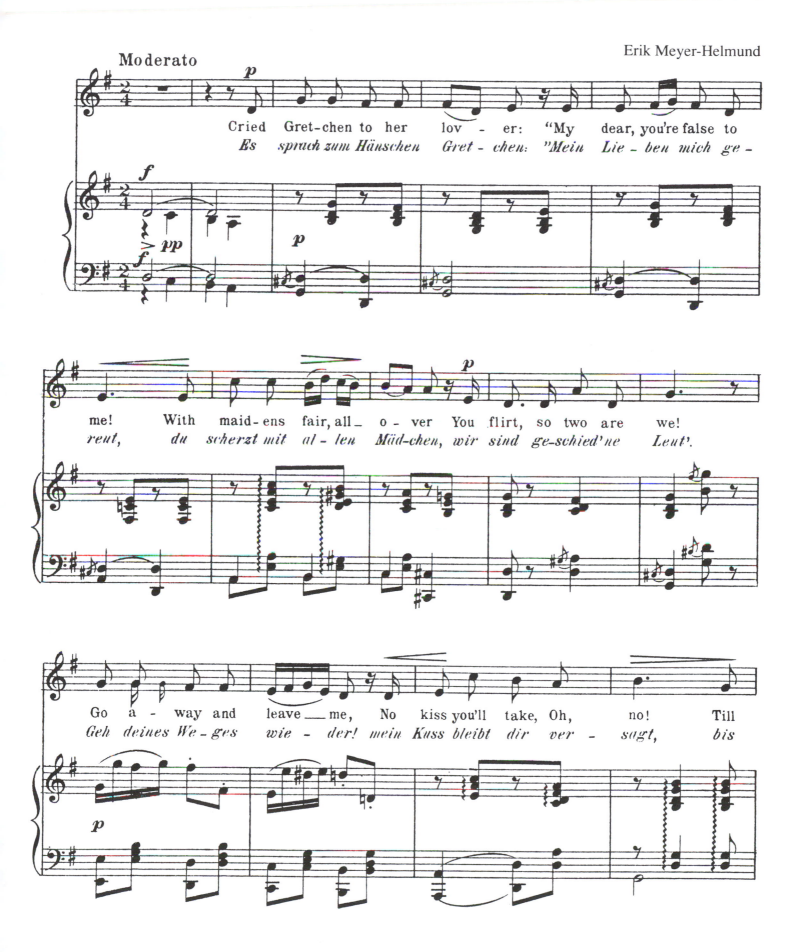

Cried Gret-chen to her lov - er: "My dear, you're false to
Es sprach zum Hänschen Gret - chen: "Mein Lie - ben mich ge -

me! With maid-ens fair, all o - ver You flirt, so two are we!
reut, du scherzt mit al - len Mäd-chen, wir sind ge-schied'ne Leut'.

Go a - way and leave me, No kiss you'll take, Oh, no! Till
Geh deines We - ges wie - der! mein Kuss bleibt dir ver - sagt, bis

One day he saw his sweet-heart Be-
Als Tags da-rauf er wie- -der den

neath the eld-er fair, And watch'd her ty-ing ap- -ples Up
Weg zur Trauten fand, sass Gret-chen auf dem Flie- -der, da-

on the branches there!
ran sie Ae- pfel band.

THE SKY ABOVE THE ROOF

Mabel Dearmer
based on Verlaine

Ralph Vaughan Williams

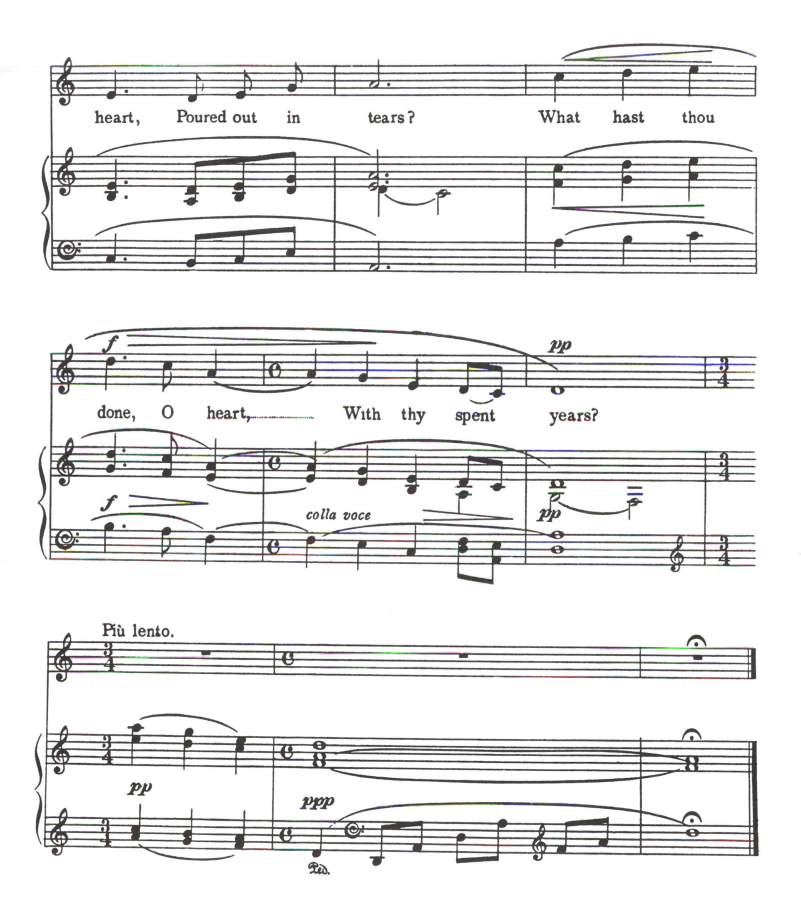

heart, Poured out in tears? What hast thou

done, O heart, With thy spent years?

THE STATUE AT CZARSKOE-SELO

Alexander Pushkin*

Cesar Cui

*English words based on the version by Charles Fonteyn Manney, Copyright, 1929, by Oliver Ditson Company.

VOLKSLIEDCHEN
(In The Garden)

Franz Ruckert

Robert Schumann

WIE MELODIEN
(A Thought Like Music)

Klaus Groth

Johannes Brahms

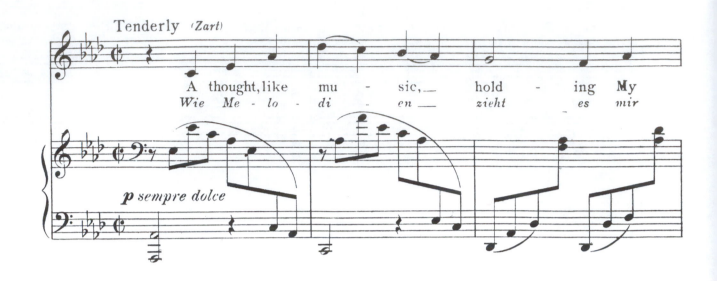

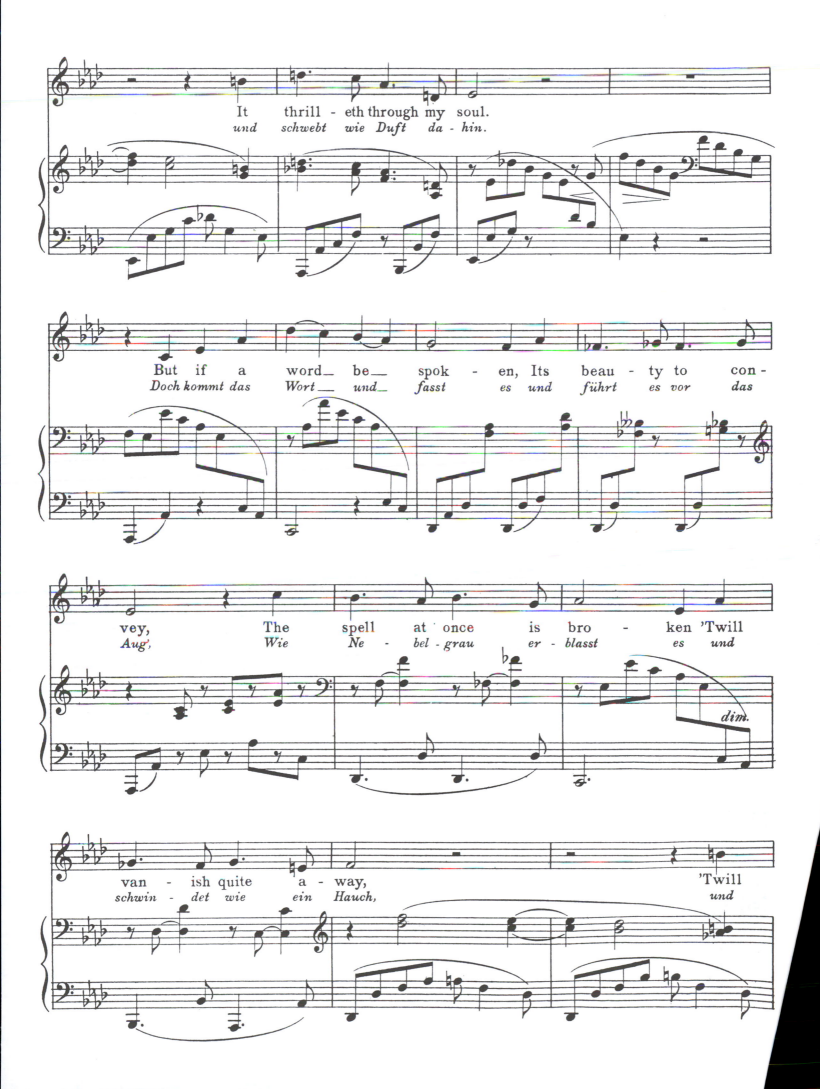

It thrill - eth through my soul.
und schwebt wie Duft da - hin.

But if a word be spok - en, Its beau - ty to con -
Doch kommt das Wort und fasst es und führt es vor das

vey, The spell at once is bro - ken 'Twill
Aug', Wie Ne - bel - grau er - blasst es und

van - ish quite a - way, 'Twill
schwin - det wie ein Hauch, und

118

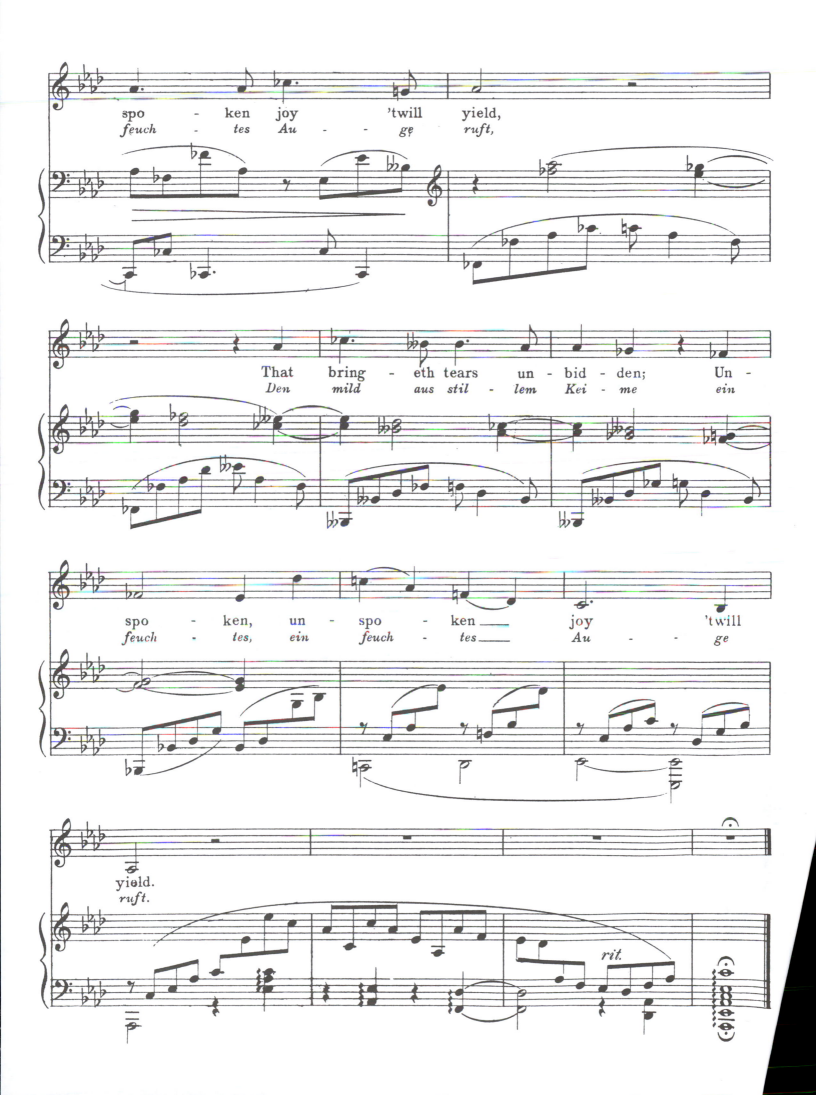

TURN THEN THINE EYES

Henry Purcell

catch-ing, catch-ing flames _____ will on __ thy torch ap-

pear, will on thy torch ap - pear, will on thy torch ap-

pear, ap-pear, will on __ thy torch ap - pear will on __ thy torch ap-

pear   pear.

WIND OF THE WESTERN SEA

Alfred Tennyson

Graham Peel

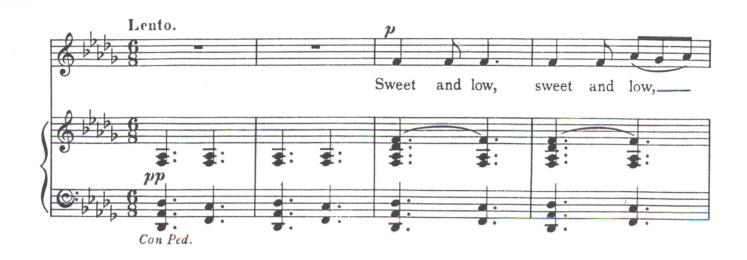

Sweet and low, sweet and low,_____

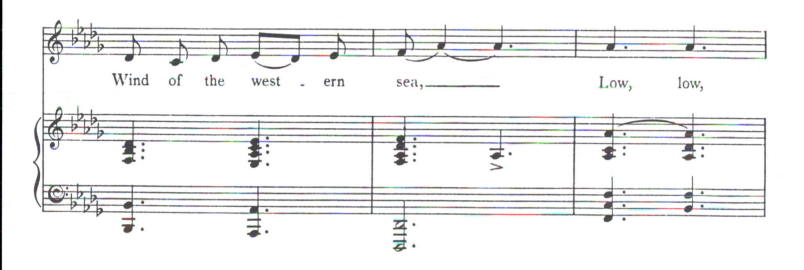

Wind of the west _ ern sea,_____ Low, low,

breathe and blow,_____ Wind of the west _ ern sea!_____

124

THIS LITTLE ROSE

Emily Dickinson*

William Roy

Moderate, and in a free, gentle manner

slightly accelerated

No-bod-y knows this lit-tle rose, It might a pil-grim

be. Did I not take it from the ways And lift it up to

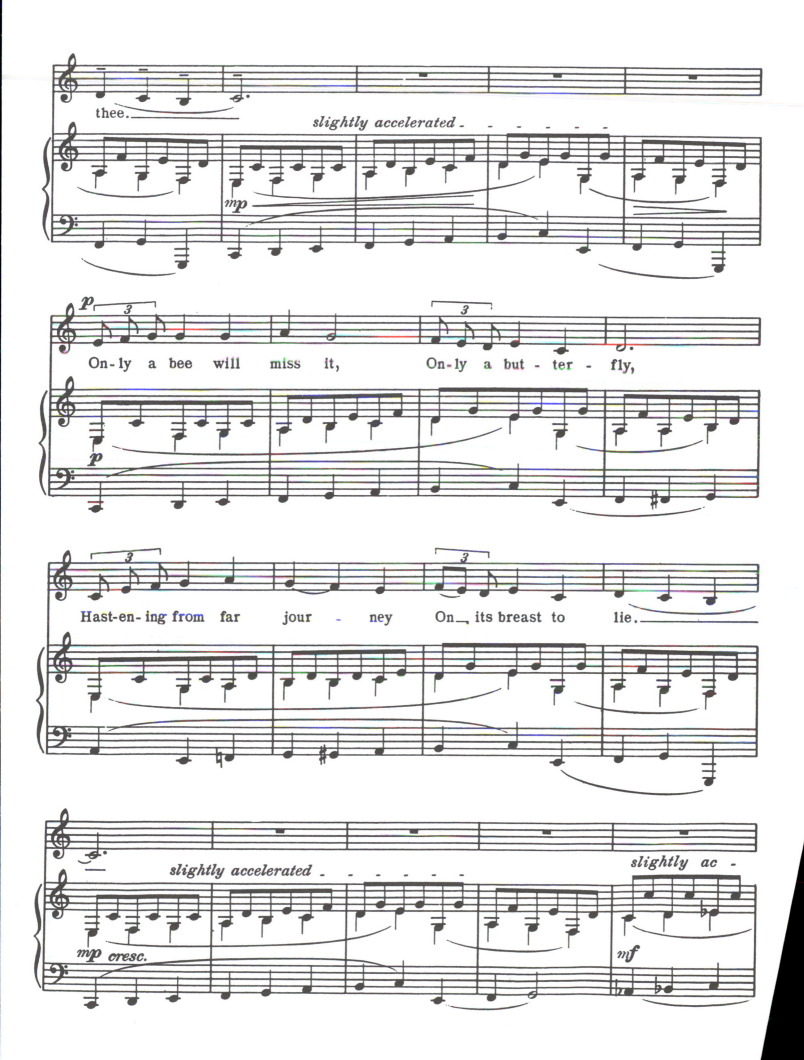

On-ly a bird will won-der,

On-ly a breeze will sigh,

Ah, lit-tle rose, how eas - y

For such as thee to die!